Learning about Fish and Mammal Species

Children's Fish and Marine Life

BABY PROFESSOR

EDUCATION KIDS

The ocean is home to many living creatures. Not all creatures that swim in the oceans are fish. There are also marine mammals like the whales, dolphins, and many others.

Here is a list of the notable differences between fish and marine mammals:

- Fish swim by moving their tails from side to side while the marine mammals swim by moving their tails up and down.

- Fish use their gills to breathe underwater while marine mammals don't have gills and they have to go up to the surface of the water in order to breathe.

- Fish are cold-blooded while marine mammals are warm-blooded.

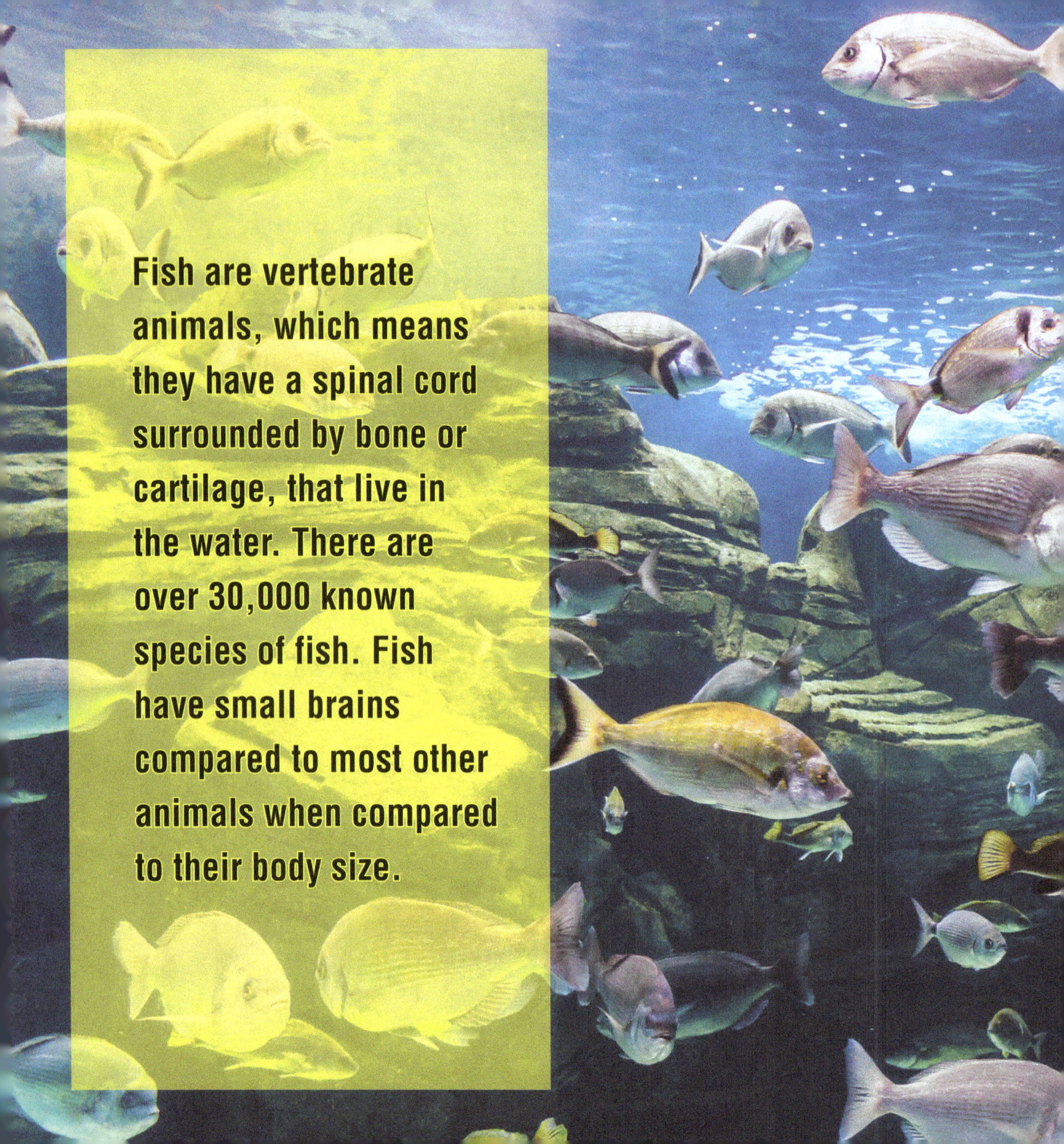

Fish are vertebrate animals, which means they have a spinal cord surrounded by bone or cartilage, that live in the water. There are over 30,000 known species of fish. Fish have small brains compared to most other animals when compared to their body size.

There are some flatfish
that use camouflage
to hide themselves
on the ocean floor.

Tuna can swim at
speeds up to 70
kph or 43 mph.

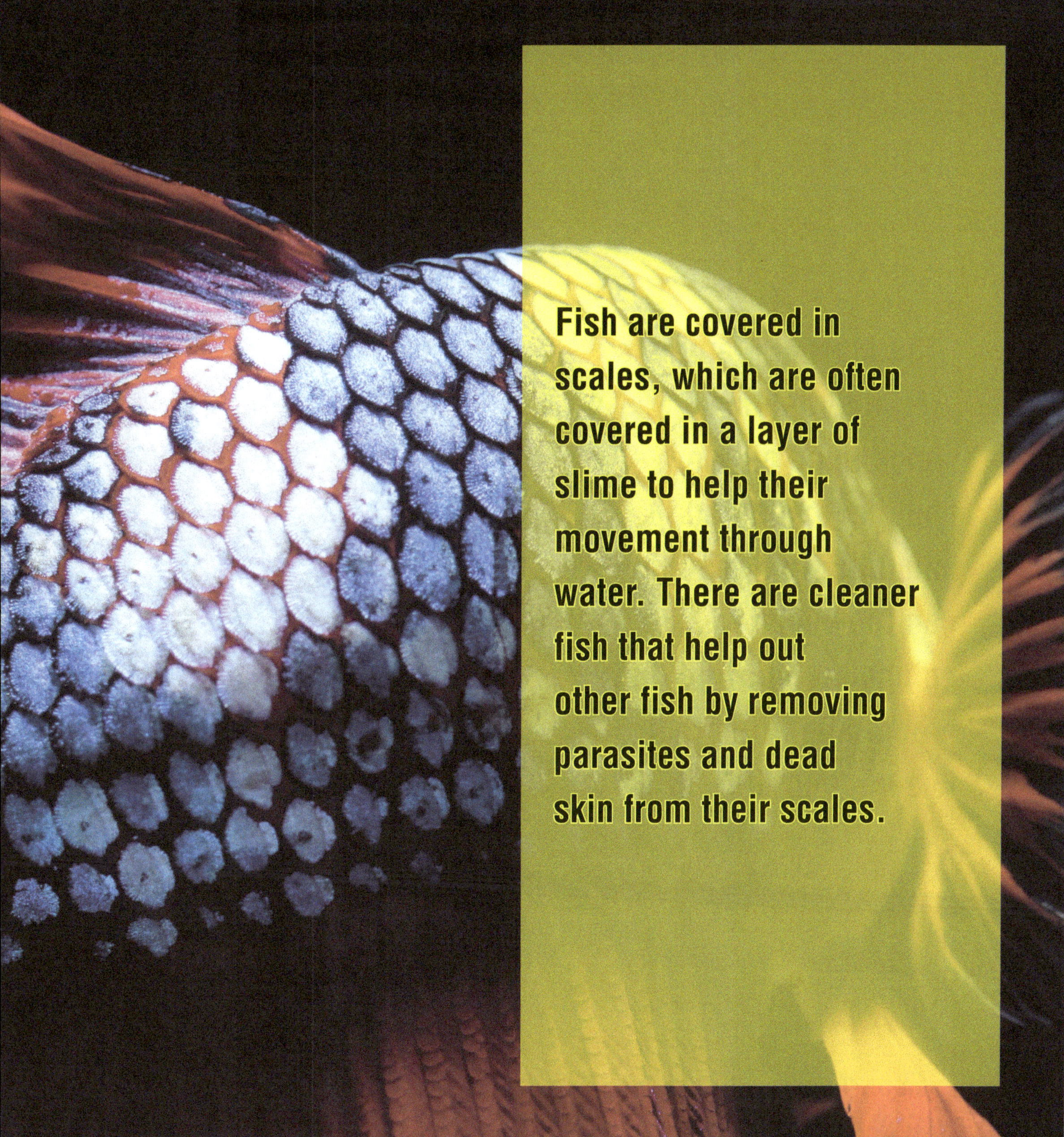

Fish are covered in scales, which are often covered in a layer of slime to help their movement through water. There are cleaner fish that help out other fish by removing parasites and dead skin from their scales.

The Marine Mammals.
Marine mammals
once lived on land,
but have adapted to
aquatic life. They rely
on the ocean to as a
place to live, find their
food, and bring their
young into the world.

Marine mammals have
many things in common
with land mammals,
like giving birth to
live young, having
mammary glands to
provide milk to feed
their young, the need
to breathe air, being
warm-blooded, and in
some cases having hair.

Marine mammals develop a thick layer of fat or blubber so they can keep their vital organs from freezing in cold water, and they consume large amounts of calories in order to maintain their body heat.

Whales do not lay eggs, unlike fish and other aquatic animals. Like humans, they carry their unborn children inside their womb until they are born.

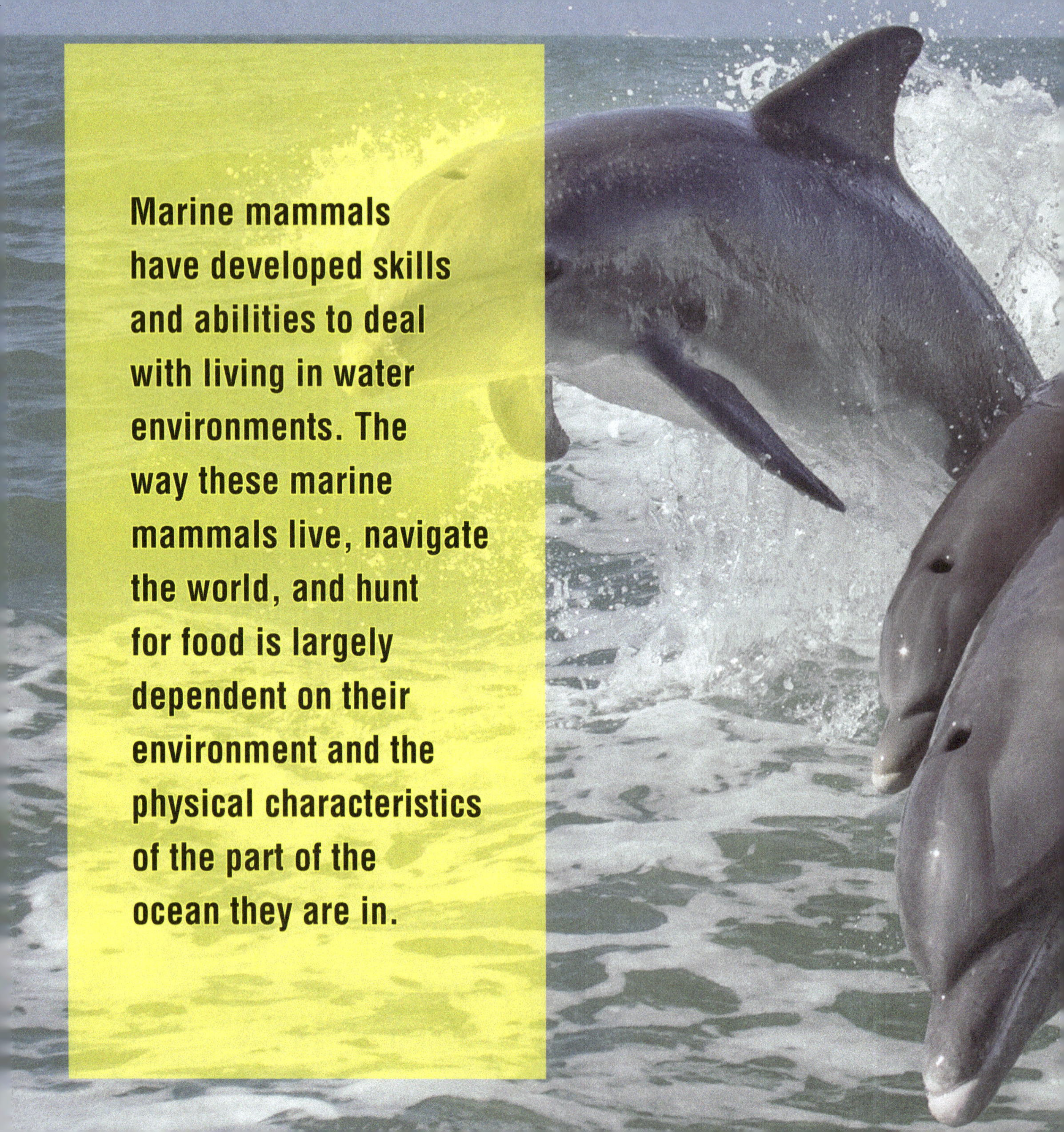

Marine mammals have developed skills and abilities to deal with living in water environments. The way these marine mammals live, navigate the world, and hunt for food is largely dependent on their environment and the physical characteristics of the part of the ocean they are in.

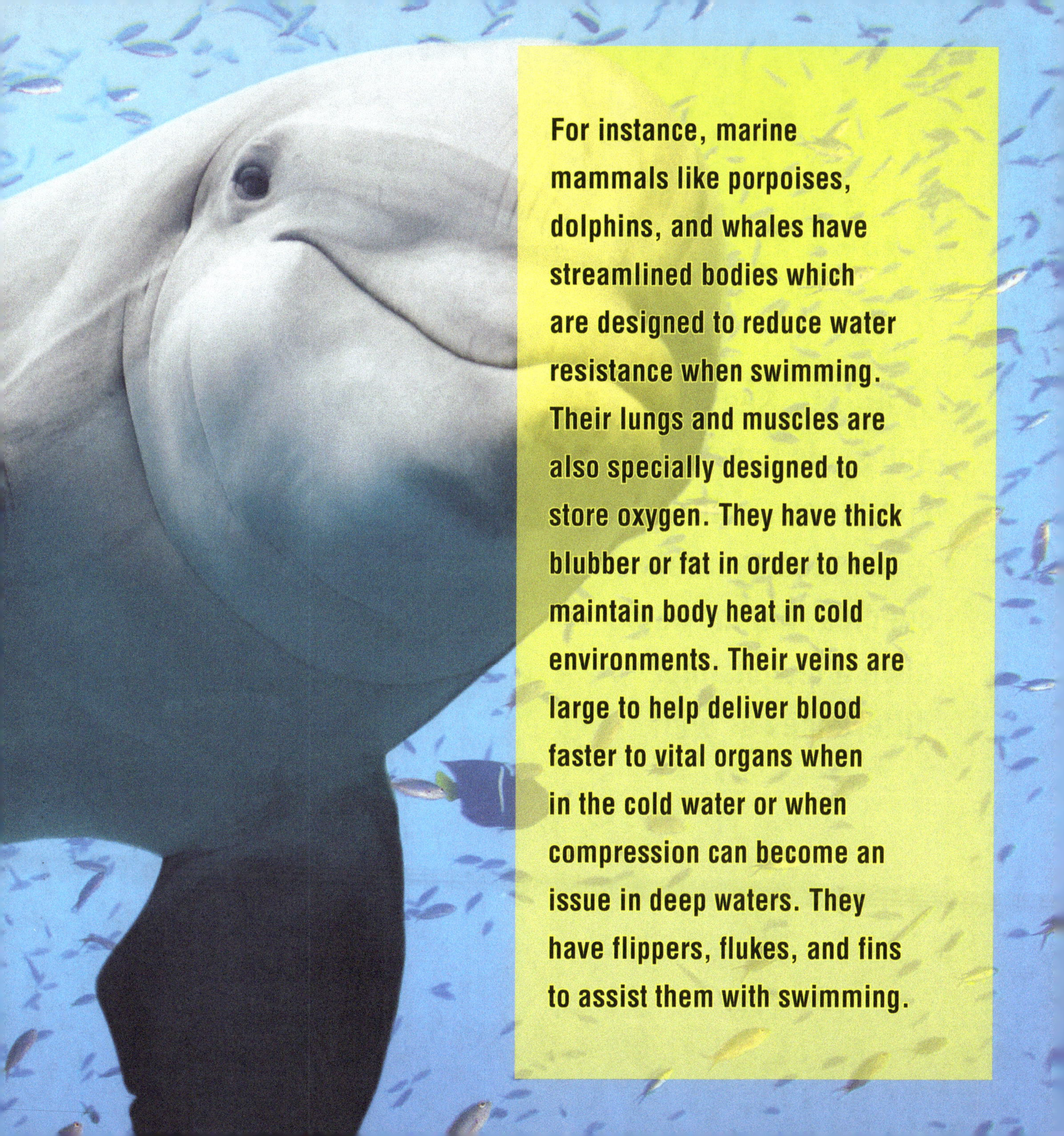

For instance, marine mammals like porpoises, dolphins, and whales have streamlined bodies which are designed to reduce water resistance when swimming. Their lungs and muscles are also specially designed to store oxygen. They have thick blubber or fat in order to help maintain body heat in cold environments. Their veins are large to help deliver blood faster to vital organs when in the cold water or when compression can become an issue in deep waters. They have flippers, flukes, and fins to assist them with swimming.

Walruses, sea lions, and seals have many similar characteristics among the separate species, but they also have a few distinct differences as well.

Walruses have a stockier build than seals and sea lions. They have two large teeth that protrude from their mouth which are similar to the teeth of a saber toothed tiger, but larger.

Seals have shorter limbs than the sea lions, with long claws. Their short limbs require them to waddle on land rather than walk. They can propel themselves through the water more effectively than sea lions due to their strong rear flippers.

Though not all marine mammals have the same biological characteristics, they all live near or in the ocean and they need the ocean for their food and for a place to live and play.

There are over 125
recorded species of
marine mammals
that have inhibited
the ocean and old
aquatic environments
of the world.

The following is a list of the of individual sub groups that are within the marine mammal family:

- **Cetaceans:** is the group of porpoises, dolphins, and whales.

- **Fissipeds:** this group includes sea otters and polar bears.

- **Pinnipeds:** is the group of walruses, sea lions, and seals.

- **Sirenians:** these are the manatees and the dugongs

Even though these animals are found throughout the world, about 40%, the highest concentration of marine mammals, are found at or around latitude 40° both south and north of the equator.

Did you enjoy reading this book?

Share this with your friends.

Visit
BABY PROFESSOR
EDUCATION KIDS
www.BabyProfessorBooks.com
to download Free Baby Professor eBooks
and view our catalog of new and exciting
Children's Books